Roger Coote

Air

Firefly

The air is all around us.
It moves even though
we can't see it.
When air moves we call it wind.

A gentle wind is called a breeze.

If the wind is very strong
we call it a gale.

The strongest wind of all is
a hurricane.
It can blow down trees and
damage houses.

Thanks to the wind we can
fly a kite . . .

13

. . . and drift along in
a big balloon.

The wind turns the sails
of a windmill . . .

. . . and pushes a sailing boat through the water.

Planes fly through the air . . .

21

. . . and so do birds . . .

23

. . . and parachutes float down
through the air to reach
the ground.

Animals and plants need air
to keep them alive.
And so do you and I.

Air is everywhere but can you see it?

Notes for adults

Children who go to school already knowing how a book 'works' have a great deal of knowledge that will help them to make the entry into reading much easier. It is far more important to share a book with a child than to try to teach him/her to read. These Firefly books aim to introduce very young children to the world around them.

Before reading this book talk about the pictures on the cover. What does your child think the book is about? Talk about the title and point to the words. Tell him/her that all books are written by authors and often illustrated by a different person. Show him/her the names of the author and illustrator.

Before reading the story look through the book and talk about the illustrations. If you wish, you can use the discussion points below, or make up your own questions. Encourage the child to tell his/her own story to the pictures. This important pre-reading skill helps children to develop an understanding of story that is essential to reading. Do let your child hold the book and give him/her time to look at the pictures before talking about them. Adults often rush in with questions far too soon.

Remember, when discussing the pictures there is no 'right' or 'wrong' guess. Accept what your child suggests and add your own ideas. You will be bringing much more knowledge to the pictures but s/he may sometimes surprise you.

After reading the book let your child explore the book on his/her own. S/he may want to return to a favourite picture, retell the story to a special toy, or just turn the pages pretending to be a reader. A joy in books comes from the reader being allowed to use them as s/he wishes and not necessarily in what an adult thinks is the 'right' way.

Discussion points

Talking about the illustrations will help your child to get more from the story. Here are some suggestions for things to discuss. The numbers refer to the pages on which the illustrations appear.

5	What is the dog doing? Why aren't the leaves green?
7	What is the little girl doing? Why are the bubbles all moving in the same direction?
9	What has happened to the umbrella? Why do you think this has happened? Why is the little girl holding her hat?
13	What is the boy doing? Have you ever flown a kite?
15	What can the children see when they are up in the air?
17	What makes the sails on the windmill turn round? What makes the bicycle wheels turn round?
18/19	How many boats can you see? Do you think the lady likes sailing?
25	Where have the people come from?
26/27	How many different animals can you find? What is the dog doing? What will the little boy do with the wheel barrow?
29	Why is the curtain moving?